A TROPICAL ADVENTURE

Name	Flight	Date	Seat
Elianny Reyes	F809	13 FEB 2023	5A

New York ➡ Dominican Republic

Gate	Boarding Time
D22	08:09

Name
Elianny Reyes

Flight   Seat
F809   5A

Date
13 FEB 2023

Gate
D22

Z Z z z

It's winter time here in the Bronx, New York. Which means it's time to travel somewhere warm and tropical. Elianny was asleep until she heard a creak at the door.

"It's time to wake up Elianny", said mom.
We have to get ready for our trip to the
Dominican Republic.

"Mami, our flight is at 8:09 am. Why are we waking up at 4 am?" asked Elianny. It is so early.

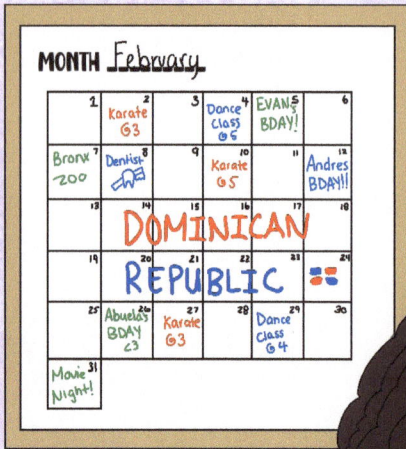

Name | Flight | Date | Seat
Elianny Reyes | F809 | 13 FEB 2023 | 5A

New York → Dominican Republic

Gate D22 | Boarding Time 08:09

Name
Elianny Reyes
Flight Seat
F809 5A
Date
13 FEB 2023
GATE D22

TAXI

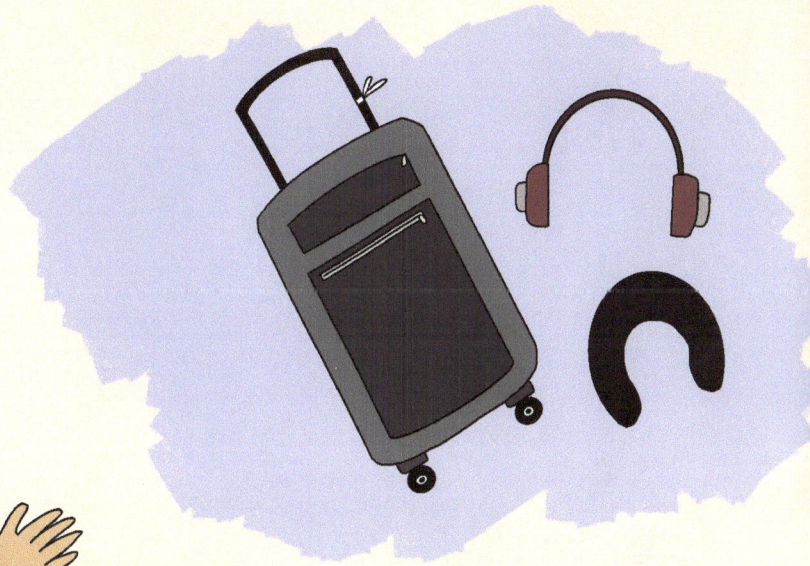

We have to get up, get ready, and double-check that we have everything prepared. We have to get ready to take the taxi too.

"What is it like over there?" asked Andres. "Are there penguins and polar bears who party all night?" "No, there are no animals like that. In the Dominican Republic, it is always warm. Polar bears and penguins can't party in the warm weather, or they will get too hot", laughed Elianny.

Instead, there are animals like pigs, chickens, iguanas, and many more. In the Dominican Republic, there is so much to explore!

SOLENODON

IGUANA

CERDO
PIG

CIGUA PALMERA
PALMCHAT
NATIONAL BIRD OF THE DOMINICAN REPUBLIC

RANA
FROG

ARAÑA
SPIDER

POLLO
CHICKEN

CABALLO
HORSE

AND MANY MORE...

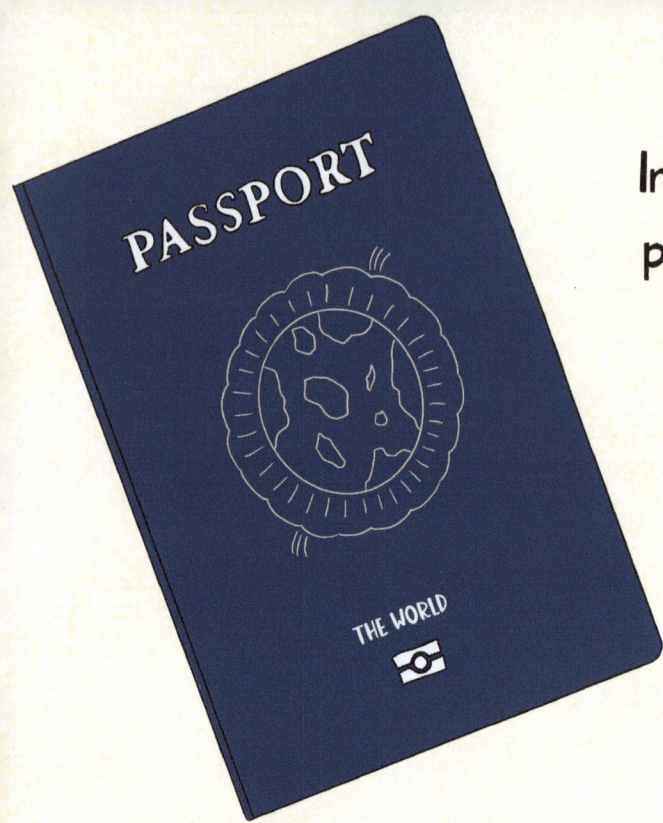

In order to go, you need a passport. A passport gives permission to travel to other countries.

Then you sit inside an airplane to fly high into the sky.

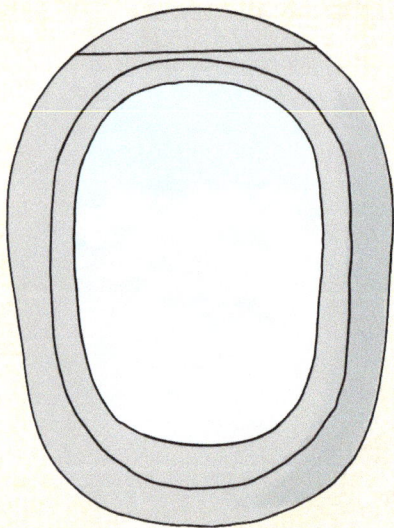

While watching the clouds pass by until it's time to land.

Dominican Republic

Quisqueya

Atlantic Ocean

Haiti

Monte Cristi

Dajabon

Mao

Sabaneta

Puerto Plata

Sosua

Nagua

Moca

Salcedo

San Francisco de Marcoris

Samana

Santiago

Elias Piña

La Vega

Bonao

Cotui

Jimani

San Juan

Neiba

Azua

Barahona

Pedernales

Isla Beata

San Cristobal

Bani

Monte Plata

Hato Mayor

El Seibo

Higüey

Santo Domingo

San Pedro De Macoris

La Romana

Punta Cana

Isla Saona

Caribbean Sea

Here is a map of places you can go. The Dominican Republic is a country on an island called Hispaniola. An island is an area of land that has water all around it.

We finally made it! Everybody started clapping in the airplane. They seemed very excited to explore the island too.

You'll always hear tropical music at the airport.
It's a way to welcome people to the island.
Music brings everyone together.

We're outside of the airport. The weather is warm and humid. There's so many people here who are waiting for their family and friends.

Tio = Uncle
Abuela = Grandmother
Primo = Cousin

We saw abuela, our primo Alex and our tio Jose. They were so excited to see us. It has been a long time since we traveled to the Dominican Republic.

This historic building is a monument located in Santiago de los Caballeros. Also known as, "Monumento a los Héroes de la Restauración."

Made in 1944, the monument symbolizes gratitude to the soldiers who battled for the Dominican's independence from Spain.

There's many different landmarks here. Each place has great sights to see.

EL CAMPO
THE COUNTRY SIDE

LAS MONTAÑAS
THE MOUNTAINS

LA CUIDAD
THE CITY

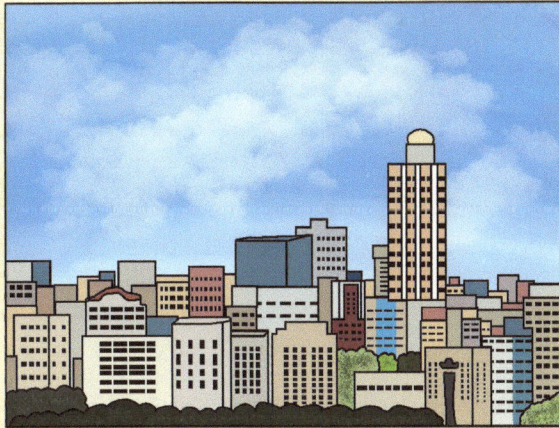

LA PLAYA
THE BEACH

EL PUEBLO
THE TOWN

EL RIO
THE RIVER

We made it to abuela's house. She lives in Piedra Blanca. It's a pueblo in the province, Monseñor Nouel. The capital of Monseñor Nouel is Bonao.

She also has her own finca. Finca means farm in Spanish. There are a lot of chickens she takes care of.

"We are hungry abuela. Tenemos hambre", Joandy said. What kind of food can we eat here?

"There are many things you can eat here Joandy. Here is a grocery list and some pesos. Alex will show you where the colmado is. When you return, I will cook a meal for you all", said abuela.

La Lista
- [ ] Platanos
- [ ] Queso Frito
- [ ] Purple Cebolla ↓ Salami Onions

Platanos = Plantains
Queso frito = Fried cheese

In the United States, we have dollars, but in the Dominican Republic we have money called pesos. We need pesos to buy our groceries and things we need.

COLMADO
COLLADO

REFRESCO

Dulce

We're at the Colmado. It's a place where a lot of people come to buy groceries and snacks. We have to make sure we buy the items on abuela's list.

FRUITS & VEGETABLES

FRUTAS Y VEGETALES

AGUACATE
AVOCADO

PLÁTANO
PLANTAIN

MANGO

COCO
COCONUT

CHINOLA
PASSION FRUIT

CARAMBOLA
STARFRUIT

BATATA
SWEET POTATO

YUCA
CASSAVA

GUANABANA
SOURSOP

LIMONCILLO
SPANISH LIME

TAMARINDO
TAMARIND

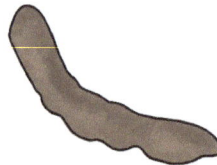

PAPAYA

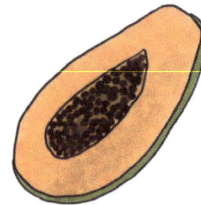

There are so many different fruits and vegetables here. They all keep the people on the island healthy and strong. These are just a few you can find. Which one would you like to try?

There are many different kinds of food to make here in the Dominican Republic. A lot of the food consists of meat, vegetables, starch, and dairy.

LA BANDERA

"La Bandera" is a traditional Dominican dish. It contains white rice, habichuelas (beans), and pollo guisado (stew chicken).

SANCOCHO

Sancocho is a famous soup full of veggies, spices, and different kinds of meat, such as beef or chicken.

LOS 3 GOLPES

This dish contains fried salami, queso frito (fried cheese), and mangú (smashed plantains).

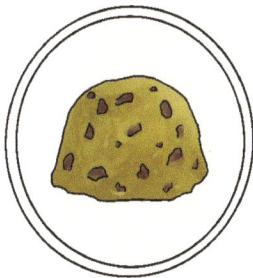

MOFONGO

Mofongo is a Caribbean dish made from plantains and is often used with chicken or pork inside.

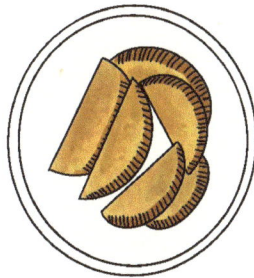

PASTELITOS

Pastelitos also known as empanadas is a fried dough dish that has many different surprises inside. It can have beef, chicken, cheese, and many more!

PASTELES EN HOJA

This dish is made with a platano dough wrapped inside a plantain leaf. It usually contains a variety of meats such as chicken, pork, and beef.

Can you guess which one abuela is going to make?

Did you guess it right? Abuela made los tres golpes. Which has smashed plantains called mangú, fried salami, and fried cheese. We also bought some yummy jugo de naranja, which is orange juice.

Dad wanted to take us to our first carnival. Before we went, he took us to the hair salon and my brothers to the barber shop.

Dominicans are well known for their smooth blow-drys and sharp haircuts!

The Dominican Carnival happens every year in February. It is a celebration to honor the country's independence. They wear colorful and creative costumes that are different every year.

Music is everywhere here! Dominicans love to dance and sing. There's genres like bachata, merengue, bolero, típico, and many more. Each genre has different dance moves.

INSTRUMENTOS
INSTRUMENTS

ACORDEÓN
ACCORDION

GÜIRA

MARACAS

DJEMBA

TAMBORA
BASS DRUM

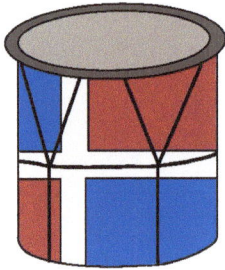

SAXOFÓN
SAXOPHONE

BONGOS

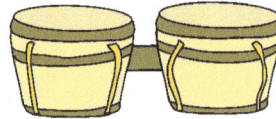

GUITARRA
GUITAR

CLAVE

BAJO ELECTRICO
ELECTRIC GUITAR

MICRÓFONO
MICROPHONE

PIANO

Here are some instruments you can find on this island. These instruments are used together to create tropical music.

There are many different sports to play in the Dominican Republic. One of the most popular sports here is baseball. You don't have to be a professional to play. The people here love to play just for fun too!

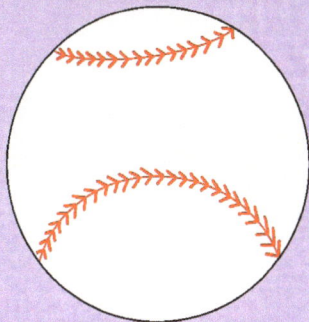

There are so many fun things to do, but my favorite part was spending time with my family. They make every moment special.

From giant insects and spiders

To chickens taking over the house

Se fue la luz

"The light went out"

Even the lights randomly turning off for an hour...

Helado = Ice Cream
Dulce = Sweet
Te llevo en mi corazón = I carry you in my heart

All of these things will always bring memories. I'm proud to be a part of the Dominican culture. Most importantly, I'll miss my abuela. Until next time República Dominicana. Te llevo en mi corazón.

New York → Dominican Republic

Name: Elianny Reyes
Flight: F809
Date: 13 FEB 2023
Seat: 5A
Gate: D22
Boarding Time: 08:09

THE END

FIN

www.ingramcontent.com/pod-product-compliance
Lightning Source LLC
LaVergne TN
LVHW072055070426
835508LV00002B/109